**DO NOT REMOVE
CARDS FROM POCKET**

**ALLEN COUNTY PUBLIC LIBRARY
FORT WAYNE, INDIANA 46802**

You may return this book to any agency, branch,
or bookmobile of the Allen County Public Library.

DEMCO

CAUSES AND CONSEQUENCES

OF

WORLD WAR II

CAUSES AND CONSEQUENCES

OF

WORLD WAR II

STEWART ROSS

RSVP
RAINTREE
STECK-VAUGHN
PUBLISHERS
The Steck-Vaughn Company

Austin, Texas

Published by Raintree Steck-Vaughn Publishers,
an imprint of Steck-Vaughn Company

Developed by the Creative Publishing Company
Editor: Deirdre McCarthy-Morrogh
Designed by Ian Winton

Raintree Steck-Vaughn Publishers staff
Project Manager: Joyce Spicer
Editor: Shirley Shalit
Electronic Production: Scott Melcer

Library of Congress Cataloging-in-Publication Data

Ross, Stewart.
    World War II / Stewart Ross.
        p.   cm. — (Causes and consequences)
    Includes bibliographical references and index.
    ISBN 0-8172-4050-0
    1. World War, 1939-1945 — Causes — Juvenile literature.
    I. Title. II. Series.
    D741.R68   1995   95-7740
    940.53'11 — dc20   CIP   AC

Printed in Hong Kong
Bound in the United States
1 2 3 4 5 6 7 8 9 0 LB 99 98 97 96 95

CONTENTS

TOTAL WAR

A GLOBAL CONFLICT

Fear of the bomber brought World War II into almost every home in Europe. It was a citizen's duty to maintain the blackout, hiding all lights that might guide a bomber to its target. This German poster warns against the danger of failing to keep the blackout.

World War II was the most widespread and destructive conflict in history. World War I, although fought by soldiers from all continents, took place largely in Europe. Huge numbers of combatants were killed and wounded in static, slogging bloodshed, but the civilian populations of most countries were rarely in direct danger from the fighting. Air warfare was in its infancy. Apart from one major naval battle, operations at sea were largely taken up with submarines and blockades.

The fighting which began about twenty years later and which became known as World War II was different in both scope and scale. It was truly worldwide, involving more countries, more people — especially civilians — and a greater area of the planet's surface than any previous war. As a result of technological developments, particularly in the aircraft industry, it was also the first total war. Nations in the front lines of the air war, such as Germany, Britain, and Japan, were obliged to divert every available resource, human, moral, and material, into the war effort. The bomber and the missile meant very few people were safe, while the parachutist and swiftly moving armored column enabled military commanders to strike deeper and faster than ever before.

World War I had been relatively straightforward, with

the powers of the Dual Alliance (Germany and Austria-Hungary) and their allies fighting against the powers of the Triple Entente (Britain, France, and Russia) and their allies. Some states entered the war and others, like Russia, left it, but no major combatant changed sides. The war began in July 1914 and ended

A U.S. Marine operates a flamethrower during the Battle of Guadalcanal, August 1942.

in November 1918. In contrast, World War II was much more complicated. Starting in the Far East in 1937, different conflicts began in different regions at different times. These gradually became absorbed into the global struggle. Countries, such as Italy, changed sides. The war in Europe ended in May 1945, while that in the Far East went on for three months longer.

CAUSES AND CONSEQUENCES

This book seeks to answer two questions. Why did World War II begin, and what were its consequences? Unfortunately, for the reasons outlined above — the war's totality, complexity, and vast extent — these questions are not easy to answer. Each country went to war at its own time and for its own reasons. For example, Japan's motives for attacking China in 1937, or the United States in 1941, were very different from

To the annoyance of many European democracies, the United States did not join World War II until it was attacked by Japan in December 1941. Even so, the war was on everyone's mind. This New York movie theater is showing captured Nazi films.

Britain's reasons for declaring war on Germany in September 1939. And the consequences of the war varied widely from country to country. Much of what follows, therefore, concerns detailed events in specific countries.

Nevertheless, since World War II was a worldwide phenomenon, it is possible to discover general conditions, common to almost all lands, which gave rise to the tensions leading to war. The example that most readily comes to mind is the economic slump that struck all industrialized nations during the 1930s. In the same way, we can discern consequences of the war that were also common to all countries. One might be the foundation of the United Nations; another might be the impact of the war's startling technological innovations, such as atomic energy.

Finally, we should not allow the complexity of the war's origins and consequences to obscure its crucial importance. Probably more than any other event this century, World War II shaped the world in which we now live.

German troops move through a Yugoslavian village in 1942. Some of the bitter divisions of this time reemerged when the country fell apart in the 1990s.

LEGACY OF THE GREAT WAR

The redrawing of the frontiers of Europe after World War I held many of the seeds of future conflict. Germany, Austria-Hungary, and Russia lost much territory, while new countries, such as Czechoslovakia and Yugoslavia, held an awkward mixture of different nationalities.

In Europe World War II began in September 1939 with an act of German aggression, an unprovoked attack on Poland. It is no coincidence that this happened barely twenty years after the ending of World War I.

In terms of loss of life, destruction, and political upheaval, there had never before been a conflict like the Great War, as the conflict of 1914-18 was known. It had, almost literally, blown the old European world apart. In 1917 Imperial Russia had succumbed to a Communist revolution. The great empires of Austria-Hungary, Turkey, and Germany had collapsed. Britain and France had survived, but the economic cost of their victory had been gigantic.

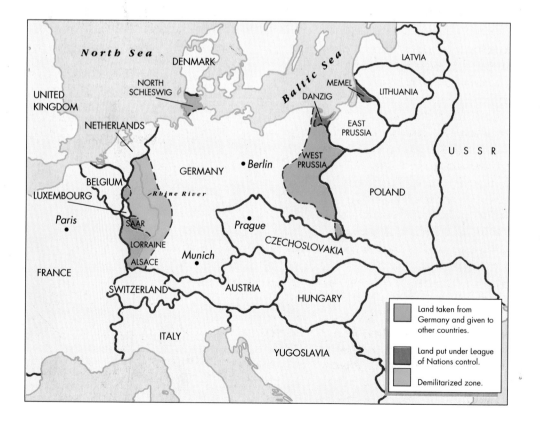

THE TREATY OF VERSAILLES

Against this background of tremendous upheaval, peace negotiators from the victorious powers met in Paris to negotiate a series of treaties with the defeated countries, the most important of which was the Treaty of Versailles. Their task was not simply to arrange peace terms, but to reorganize a shattered world and establish a mechanism whereby such a terrible conflict could never reoccur. They were guided by "Fourteen Points" suggested by America's President Woodrow Wilson. These included such idealistic principles as reducing armaments and economic barriers, and allowing people to decide to which nation they belonged. Tragically, there was another principle in the minds of some of the negotiators: that those believed responsible for starting the war, particularly the Germans, ought to be punished. Too late did people discover that blame and punishment were incompatible with lasting peace.

The Treaty of Versailles was extremely hard on Germany, which took no part in the negotiations and had no say in the final terms. The nation was stripped of all its overseas colonies, which were seized by the victors under the pretense of looking after them for the League of Nations (see page 13). European territory was taken away, too. For example, Alsace-Lorraine was returned to France, West Prussia went to Poland, while the Saar and the port of Danzig, both of which were largely German-speaking, were put under the supervision of the League of Nations. This meant that a portion of Germany was split off with a Polish "corridor" running between. The Rhineland was demilitarized. Three million Sudetenland German speakers found themselves in newly established Czechoslovakia

The signing of the peace treaty with Germany in Versailles' Hall of Mirrors, painted by Sir William Orpen. The German delegate, Dr. Johannes Bell, seated with his back to the artist, signs the treaty watched by the victorious Allies. Opposite him in the center, seated from left to right, are President Woodrow Wilson of the United States, President Georges Clemenceau of France, and Prime Minister Lloyd George of Britain.

and a further million in Poland. Germany had to accept sole responsibility for starting the war. So it could never repeat what it had done, its armed forces were limited to an army of 100,000, with no armored vehicles, no airforce, and a small navy with a maximum of six battleships. Finally, the victors demanded that Germany pay $56 billion to them in reparations — compensation for war damage.

It is not difficult to see the seeds of future conflict in these terms. They were unnecessarily harsh and unrealistic. Although Germany was still the largest economic power in Europe, it could not hope to pay the vast reparations. German people found themselves living beyond German frontiers. The limit of 100,000 troops, the Germans claimed, was insufficient to maintain internal security and certainly inadequate to protect their country from aggression.

Shortly after the end of World War I the German economy collapsed. By 1923 unemployment was high and inflation soaring out of control. Here, a German soup kitchen serves food to the unemployed and hungry in 1931.

And it was both unfair and unwise to force the Germans to accept that they alone had caused the war. As with almost all wars, the origins of World War I were as complex as they were controversial.

The peace settlements of 1919-20 had other weaknesses. The redrawing of frontiers and establishment of new countries — Yugoslavia and Czechoslovakia — created as many problems as they solved. Italy complained that it had not received the territory it had been promised. Austria and Hungary, whose populations had suddenly been reduced from 22 million to 6.5 million and from 21 million to 7.5 million respectively, faced massive economic problems. The Turks and Arabs felt cheated, too.

Today in . . . Versailles the disgraceful Treaty is being signed. Do not forget it! The German people will with unceasing labor press forward to reconquer the place among nations to which it is entitled. Then will come vengeance for the shame of 1919.

From Deutsche Zeitung *newspaper,* 1919.

THE LEAGUE OF NATIONS

All this might not have mattered if the new international organization established by the Peace of Paris, the League of Nations, had been able to keep a watchful eye on world affairs and settle disputes evenhandedly. Based at Geneva, Switzerland, the League's twin aims were to encourage international cooperation and maintain peace through "collective security," meaning working together. Almost from the start, however, the League proved a toothless tiger. A serious drawback was that three important nations had no part in it. Germany, because of its war record, and the new Soviet Union (USSR), because it was Communist, were left out. Worried at their country's growing worldwide commitments, the United States Senate refused to ratify the Treaty of Versailles, thereby preventing the U.S. from joining the League. Another of the League's major problems was that it had no means of enforcing its decisions, other than the imposition of economic sanctions of doubtful effectiveness. In the end, as the Japanese, Italians, and Germans were to discover, if a country chose to ignore the League's pronouncements, there was nothing the League could do about it.

The settlements that brought the Great War to a close certainly did not make a second war inevitable. But they did leave important problems unresolved and a large reservoir of bitterness — certain recipes for future trouble. No wonder the great French general, Marshal Foch, called the Versailles settlement nothing more than a "twenty-year cease-fire."

The Members of the League undertake to respect and preserve as against external aggression the territorial integrity and existing political independence of all Members of the League.

From the Covenant of the League of Nations, 1919.

TURMOIL IN ASIA

THE RISE OF JAPAN

During the thirties, Japan began expanding its empire in the East, taking first Manchuria in 1931-32, and then other key parts of China throughout the decade.

World War II began in two unstable regions of the world, Europe and the Far East. In Europe an aggressive Germany was the focal point. In Asia that role was played by Japan.

Japan had been the first Far Eastern country to industrialize, and by 1918 things were looking good for that nation. Japan had a powerful, modern navy, a strong army and, helped by the problems other trading nations had experienced on account of World War I, was making great advances as an economic power. Between 1914 and 1918, for example, the tonnage of her merchant fleet had doubled. There were encouraging political developments, too. In 1925 all adult males were given the vote and it seemed as if the country would continue steadily down the road to a full-blown democracy. Then things began to go wrong.

Some of the most influential groups in the country, particularly the military, were very conservative. They were not happy with Japan's movement toward democracy, nor did they approve of what they saw as the government's "soft" policy toward their weak and divided neighbor, China. Whenever they could, the conservatives discredited the government. This was made easier by the number of corruption scandals.

SOVIET UNION

MONGOLIA

MANCHURIA

• Vladivostock

Sea of Japan

KOREA

JAPAN

• Tokyo

Yellow Sea

CHINA

East China Sea

Shanghai •

PACIFIC OCEAN

OKINAWA

IWO JIMA

FORMOSA

South China Sea

MARIANA ISLANDS

FRENCH INDOCHINA

PHILIPPINE ISLANDS

GUAM

CAROLINA ISLANDS

BORNEO

CELEBES

NEW GUINEA

JAVA

TIMOR

Areas controlled by Japan in 1931.

Areas controlled by Japan in 1941.

Japanese air force pilots receive a final briefing before a flight in the 1930s. Since the 1920s the Japanese had built up the enormous naval and air forces that would be capable of dominating the Far East. However, they suffered from a shortage of base materials and oil fuel, a situation that made Japan vulnerable to an American oil embargo.

Economic problems brought matters to a head. First, the golden economic conditions of 1914-21 could not last. Europe recovered and began to claw back some of the markets it had lost. Second, beginning in 1929, world trade went into a major and prolonged recession. Japan's exports of raw silk were particularly hard hit, the 1932 price falling to one fifth of that in 1923. Farmers, businessmen, and merchants all suffered. Poverty and discontent stalked the land.

In this gloomy climate, the army decided to move. In 1931, without government permission and in defiance of the League of Nations, it invaded the northern Chinese province of Manchuria to preserve Japanese interests there. When Prime Minister Tsuyoshi Inukai objected, he was assassinated. His replacement felt obliged to support the army's action, and throughout the 1930s Japan fell increasingly under military control. Manchuria was declared to be the independent country of Manchukuo, although in reality it was a Japanese puppet state. In 1933, following a recommendation from the Assembly of the League of Nations that it should pull out of Manchuria, Japan left the League. The following year Japan renounced the Washington and London Naval Agreements by which it had agreed to limit the size of its navy. In 1936, fearing the might of the USSR and sensing that Japan had common interests with Fascist Germany, Germany and Japan signed an anti-Communist agreement known as the Anti-Comintern Pact.

At home, Japanese soldiers were given key jobs, left-wing groups were banned, censorship and propaganda dictated the output of the media, which praised military and heroic deeds, and armaments expanded. By 1938 about 3,800 aircraft a year were being built. Three years later Japan had the world's third largest navy and an army of about 1.7 million men. Long before this, Japan's leaders had begun to look around for areas of military expansion.

WAR IN CHINA

TOP SECRET

This dispatch is to be considered as a war warning. An aggressive move by Japan is expected in the next few days. The number and equipment of Japanese troops and the organization of naval task forces indicate an amphibious expedition against either the Philippines, Thai or Kra peninsula, and possibly Borneo. Exercise an appropriate defensive deployment.

A U.S. diplomatic dispatch of November 27, 1941

China was the obvious target for Japanese aggression. Since the revolution of 1911, the country had been in chaos. After a period of control by various regional warlords, by about 1928 the Nationalists (GMD) under Jiang Jieshi (Chiang Kai-shek) had emerged as the major power. However, they were opposed by Mao Zedong's Communists and a long civil war followed. It was this internal division that the Japanese sought to exploit in July 1937 when a skirmish between patrolling Japanese soldiers and a Chinese unit on the Marco Polo Bridge outside Peking gave them an excuse to launch a full-scale invasion of China. As this war was still going on when fighting began in Europe two years later, and the Sino-Japanese war became part of the worldwide conflict, it has been argued by some that the Marco Polo Bridge incident really began World War II.

In vain the GMD and Communists made an uneasy alliance to try to resist the Japanese. Nanking fell in December and by the end of 1938 the invader controlled most of northeast China, as well as the eastern seaboard. The Japanese advance was accompanied by horrifying displays of violence, with soldiers publicly competing to kill the most Chinese.

Although the occupation of vast areas of China was a staggering achievement, it did not bring the Japanese the raw materials — in particular rubber, oil, bauxite, and tin — that their industry so badly needed. In response to this, they set up first a New Order in East Asia, then the Greater East Asia Co-prosperity Sphere. These were really plans for a Japanese-controlled common market, extended by force if necessary. The outbreak of war in Europe gave the Japanese an ideal opportunity for further expansion while the attention of the Far Eastern colonial powers (France, Britain, and the Netherlands) was focused elsewhere.

DISPUTES WITH THE WEST

In 1940 the Japanese asked Britain to close the Burma Road, by which supplies from the United States and Britain had been reaching Jiang Jieshi overland. The British had no wish to add to their troubles in Europe by stirring up Japanese hostility, and so they obliged. However, on September 27, 1940, Japan allied itself to Germany and Italy in a Tripartite Pact. With U.S. backing, Britain reopened the Burma Road. When Hitler invaded the USSR in June 1941, Japan occupied Indochina (now Vietnam, Cambodia, and Laos), with the permission of the French Vichy government. In response, Britain, the Netherlands, and the U.S. placed heavy embargoes on trade with Japan, the most damaging of which was a total ban on oil exports.

The Japanese were now in a corner. They had either to back down, or seize the supplies they required by force. Too proud to give way and realizing that further conquest would almost certainly draw a military response from Britain and the U.S., they decided to strike first. The result was an unannounced twin attack, against the British in Malaya and against the U.S. Pacific Fleet in the Hawaiian base of Pearl Harbor. The Japanese planes went in on December 7, 1941, and suddenly it seemed the whole world was at war.

Fearing that war with the U.S. was inevitable, the Japanese launched a surprise air attack on the American naval base at Pearl Harbor, Hawaii, on December 7, 1941. Fortunately for the U.S., the Pacific Fleet's three aircraft carriers were at sea. Nevertheless 90 percent of the American air and sea power in the mid-Pacific was destroyed or immobilized. The battleship USS California, seen here, was later refloated and rebuilt and saw action again later in the war.

THE ADVANCE OF FASCISM

THE RISE OF HITLER

A German poster of 1923 displays France as a crazed militaristic woman, grabbing all she can from the rich Rhineland.

The years immediately following World War I were full of turmoil. There was civil war in Russia, where the Whites, backed by the Western democracies, tried to overthrow the Communist Bolsheviks, or Reds. There was an economic downturn in most Western countries, causing unemployment, hardship, and political discontent. In Germany this led to attempted coups by both left- and right-wing groups. One of the latter, Adolf Hitler's National Socialists, were later to feature on the world stage rather more prominently. In 1923, when the French, who were struggling with economic and political problems of their own, found that reparation payments were not being maintained, they occupied the Ruhr, Germany's richest industrial region, and helped themselves to German raw materials. After refusing to join the League of Nations, the United States withdrew into isolationism. In 1922 an extreme right-wing party known as the Fascists came to power in Italy. Fascism is a dictatorial political system in which the state is the supreme source of law, order, and national life. Ordinary people are given few rights and are expected to submit to the will of the state. In Italy, where Fascism originated, the Fascists were led by Benito

Achtet auf den rechten Weg!

Reaktion
Jn's neue Deutschland

Bolschewismus und Untergang →

Deutsche demokratische Partei

"Take the Right Way!" — a campaign poster for the German Democratic Party, 1930. As the depression deepened in the early 1930s, so Germany's democratic system of government came under increasing strain. Ironically, it survived long enough to bring Hitler and his Nazis to power in 1933, after which it was swept away.

Mussolini, who soon became the country's dictator — *Il Duce* (the leader). As we have seen, both China and Japan also faced serious internal difficulties.

By the later 1920s, however, conditions were improving, particularly in Europe and the United States. A general mood of optimism emerged. World trade and manufacturing rose, lowering unemployment, raising living standards, and encouraging political stability. Germany was admitted to the League of Nations in 1926, and the Dawes and Young Plans (1924 and 1929) eased the burden of reparations. The French withdrew from the occupied region of the Ruhr in 1925. In the same year the Locarno Pact, accepting Germany as an equal partner, guaranteed western

No! National Socialist Germany wants peace because of its fundamental convictions. And it wants peace also owing to the realization of the simple primitive fact that no war would . . . alter the distress in Europe . . . Germany needs peace and desires peace!

Hitler in a speech to the Reichstag, 1935.

European frontiers. Three years later 65 nations signed the Kellogg-Briand Pact, renouncing war as an instrument of policy.

THE GREAT DEPRESSION

A soup kitchen for the unemployed of Chicago, 1930. The worldwide economic slump that began with the collapse of the New York stock exchange in October 1929 spread rapidly. As unemployment rose, so did political discontent, leading to the rise of extremist movements of both the left and right.

In October 1929 the world economy suddenly went into reverse, signaled by a dramatic slump on the U.S. stock market (the Wall Street crash). Banks called in their loans from overseas as well as from domestic customers, companies went bankrupt, and unemployment rose once more. In the U.S., industrial production fell by 50 percent. In the established democracies, such as Britain and the U.S., the slump brought down governments, but it did not damage the political system itself. Elsewhere, particularly in Germany, the long-term political consequences of economic collapse were more serious than the collapse itself.

As unemployment in Germany rose from one and a half million in the middle of 1929 to over six million by

NEHME JEDE
ARBEIT GLEICH
WELCHER ART
SOFORT AN.

The slump of the early 1930s was worldwide. The notice around the neck of this young German reads, "I will take on work of any kind immediately."

the early months of 1932, voters became increasingly disenchanted with the traditional parties. In desperation, a large number of them turned to the National Socialists, or Nazis, and their charismatic leader Adolf Hitler. The Nazis promised work and a restoration of national pride, overturning the humiliation of Versailles. To many Germans Hitler gave the impression of being just the man they needed — a strong, determined, and efficient leader who knew exactly where he was going. Quite legally, although his party did not have an absolute majority in the German parliament, the Reichstag, he became chancellor of Germany on January 30, 1933.

At once Hitler set about securing his authority. Using strong-arm tactics, he got an Enabling Law through the Reichstag, giving him huge personal power. Opposition groups were eliminated, concentration camps were set up for "undesirables," rearmament was begun, and the army was brought under the Führer's (leader's) personal control. Fueled by government expenditure, the German economy soon started to recover. A scapegoat for all ills was found in the Jews, who were persecuted with increasing severity. All this

Hitler takes the salute during the Nazi Party rally at Nuremberg in 1935. Hitler staged a number of similar extravagant spectacles during the 1930s.

went hand in hand with an aggressive foreign policy.

From the first Hitler had made it clear that he regarded the Treaty of Versailles as a shameful document not worth the paper it was written on. His aim was to make all Germans — a people he proclaimed as the world's master race — part of a powerful new Germany, at the heart of a great empire known as the Third Reich. If force was needed to do this, he had warned in his book *Mein Kampf*, then force would be used. Before long, it was clear that these were not idle threats.

A POLICY OF APPEASEMENT

It is easy, and too simple, to blame Hitler for the outbreak of World War II in Europe. Moreover, history is concerned with explanation rather than blame. Therefore, the sort of questions we ought to ask are: Why was a man with Hitler's opinions able to come to power, and why, once he was in power, did the leaders of other countries let him get away with so much before they attempted to stop him? The answer to the first, as we have seen, lay in the condition of Germany in 1932-33 and the attitude of the people. For the answer to the second, we need to examine what was going on in the rest of Europe at the time, and understand the meaning of "appeasement."

The countries who most feared Nazi aggression were Germany's immediate neighbors, Poland, Czechoslovakia, and France, and the Communist

A Nazi storm-trooper ensures that no one breaks his party's boycott of Jewish shops, April 1933. The party's extreme racism, particularly its anti-Semitism, was making itself felt only months after Hitler became chancellor in January 1933.

German-speaking Czechs turn out to welcome Nazi troops entering the Sudetenland in October 1938. From the beginning Hitler announced that he wished all Germans to belong to his Third Reich, a policy that was widely popular among German speakers living in neighboring countries.

USSR under the dictatorship of Josef Stalin. Poland signed a ten-year nonaggression treaty with Germany in 1934 and Czechoslovakia made a defensive pact with the USSR. Stalin took his country into the League of Nations and came to an agreement with France as well as with Czechoslovakia. France completed the Maginot Line, a huge defensive wall of fortresses along its frontier with Germany. All these arrangements were flawed. The Maginot line did not cover the whole of France's eastern frontier to the north with Belgium. Also few Western nations trusted the Communist USSR, which many democrats believed was more dangerous than Nazi Germany. For his part, Stalin did not trust the West. He thought countries like Britain and France looked favorably on Hitler as a weapon with which to fight Communism.

Until 1938 the policy of France and, particularly, Britain towards Germany was one of appeasement. This meant agreeing to Hitler's demands, as long as they were not too extravagant, rather than plunging Europe into another war. The justifications for such a policy were various: it was a useful way of buying time while the West rearmed; as it was widely agreed that the Treaty of Versailles had been too harsh, appeasement was a form of compensation, a way of righting past injustices; to those who remembered the horrors and slaughter of the Great War, almost anything was better than risking another war; the Fascist Nazis, for whom several Western politicians had a sneaking admiration, were a useful counterbalance to the threat of Communism. Hitler first made his views clear in 1933 when he left the World Disarmament Conference and the League of Nations. Against the direct order of the Treaty of Versailles, he then tried to unite Germany with Austria, a process known as *Anschluss*, but was prevented by the prompt action of Britain, France, and Italy. This was the last time that all three of the old World War I allies acted together.

THE OPENING MOVES

In 1935, when Mussolini defied the League of Nations and started his conquest of Abyssinia (now Ethiopia), Britain and France failed to act. The message to all would-be aggressors seemed clear. It was reinforced in the same year when Hitler negotiated with Britain, in violation of the Treaty of Versailles, to be allowed to build up his navy. After receiving overwhelming popular support in a plebiscite, Germany reoccupied the Saarland. The year 1936 marked an important stage in the drawing up of future battle lines. Hitler and Mussolini, who had hitherto been hostile toward each other, formed the Rome-Berlin Axis and Germany signed the Anti-Comintern Pact (see page 15) with Japan. Italy joined the pact the following year. In March 1936 German troops marched unopposed into the Rhineland, an area demilitarized by the Treaties of Versailles and Locarno. When civil war broke out in Spain, Hitler and Mussolini were quite open in their support for the right-wing Nationalists led by General Francisco Franco.

By December 1937 (when Mussolini took Italy out of the League of Nations), although peace was threatened by Fascist aggression in Europe and the Sino-Japanese war in the Far East, the world was still a long way from global conflict. A year later, however, the situation was far more grave. First, after bullying

The strike force of the Blitzkrieg — Junkers 87 "Stuka" dive bombers. The planes were fitted with sirens to make them sound more terrifying as they dived into action.

and threatening the Austrian government, in March 1938 Hitler sent troops into Austria and united the country with his own. Once again Versailles had been ignored and no one had done anything about it. Hitler then turned his attention to Czechoslovakia.

When the Czech state had been set up in 1919, it contained within its frontiers three million German speakers in the Sudetenland. Encouraged by Nazi propaganda, the Sudeten Germans were now campaigning for union of their part of Czechoslovakia, the Sudetenland, with Germany. Hitler threatened war on their behalf, saying it was the "last territorial claim which I have to make in Europe." While preparing for war, Britain and France tried desperately to preserve peace. Three times British prime minister Neville Chamberlain flew to meet Hitler. Eventually, at a conference held in Munich on September 29, 1938, France and Britain told the Czechs that they were not prepared to fight Germany over the Sudetenland. It was agreed that German troops could occupy the Sudetenland, while Britain and France would guarantee to protect the rest of Czechoslovakia. Hitler had his way, appeasement had preserved European peace and a delighted Chamberlain arrived home to declare that he had secured "peace for our time."

How horrible, fantastic, incredible it is that we should be digging trenches . . . here because of a quarrel in a faraway country between people of whom we know nothing!

Neville Chamberlain in a broadcast about the Sudetenland problem, September 28, 1938.

The British prime minister, Neville Chamberlain, visits Munich in 1938. His policy of appeasement toward Hitler is generally thought to have been mistaken, but his defenders claim that by not immediately responding to aggression he bought Britain time in which to prepare for war.

MUNICH TO PEARL HARBOR

FROM PEACE CONFERENCE
TO WORLD WAR

German troops enter Prague, the capital of Czechoslovakia, in March 1939. While some greeted the invaders with Nazi salutes, the overall reaction was one of anger and dismay. The Czech president, Emil Hacha, had been forced to accept a German protectorate, with Hitler threatening to bomb Prague if he did not agree.

It was soon frighteningly clear that the Munich agreement had settled nothing, apart from the fate of Czechoslovakia. The country had lost 70 percent of its heavy industry and its only defensible frontier. Internal turmoil followed, which was settled when, under the pretext of restoring law and order, German troops marched into the Czech provinces of Bohemia and Moravia. In theory they had been invited in by the Czech president, who had been told that the ancient and beautiful city of Prague would be bombed if he objected. In reality, therefore, when at the same time Hungary helped itself to the southern part of the country and Poland occupied a small area in the north,

Czechoslovakia had been conquered. In the same month Hitler took over the Lithuanian city of Memel, once a part of German East Prussia.

Britain and France both protested the fates of Czechoslovakia and Memel, but they were still not prepared to fight. What they did do was make public and concrete guarantees of Poland's independence. But what was Hitler, who had his eyes on the German-speaking free city of Danzig within the Polish corridor, to make of these guarantees? Time and again he had been warned by the Western democracies, only to find that when it came to the crunch, they backed down. Surely, he reasoned, they would do the same over Poland? But first, just to make sure that if war came he would not have to fight it on two fronts, he needed an important treaty.

The Nazi-Soviet Pact of August 22, 1939, negotiated by Foreign Ministers Joachim von Ribbentrop and Vyacheslav Molotov, was as blatantly cynical an agreement as one could find. The ideas and aims of the two countries — Fascism and Communism — were at either end of the political range. Their leaders hated and mistrusted each other. Yet just then war was in the interest of neither of them. Hitler wished to be free to tackle Poland without the USSR coming to his

Troops of the defeated Polish army in September 1939. Although Britain had formally guaranteed Poland's independence six days before, Hitler's troops invaded the country on September 1, 1939. The Poles were ill-prepared to face the high-speed attack of the Panzer corps and when on September 17 the Soviets also invaded, their resistance soon crumbled.

enemy's aid. Stalin, whose country was technologically backward and recently had been seriously weakened by the removal of leading personnel, was ill-prepared to take on the might of Germany. Stalin played for time. The result was the pact, in which they agreed to divide Poland and not fight each other.

The Poles refused to negotiate over Danzig, and Hitler invaded on September 1, 1939. Poland was swiftly overrun. By the time of Poland's surrender, however, Germany was involved in a major European war. Adhering to the terms of their agreements with Poland, Britain and France declared war on Germany on September 3. Although the USSR and the United States kept out of the main conflict at this stage, the Soviets invaded Finland on November 30 and were expelled from the League. The USSR was also in conflict with Japan in the Far East.

The next wave of countries became involved the following spring, when Germany invaded first Denmark and Norway (April 1940), then Belgium, the Netherlands, and Luxembourg (May 1940). In June, when Mussolini was sure that things were going Hitler's way, he brought Italy into the war. With this move the conflict spread to the eastern Mediterranean and North Africa, with Italian invasions of Somalia,

The Italian dictator, Benito Mussolini, (center) talking with officers of the German High Command on the Eastern Front in 1941. Although the Fascist states of Germany and Italy were united in a Pact of Steel (May 22, 1939), the hearts of many Italians were not in the war and Hitler found his Italian allies an increasing liability.

Greece, and Egypt. In September, Germany, Italy, and Japan made their Tripartite Pact, bringing a global conflict nearer. The pact was joined by Hungary, Romania, and Slovakia in November, and by Bulgaria the following March.

In 1941 the war was spreading worldwide with the linking of the eastern and western wars. During the first half of the year fighting expanded into the Middle East and along the coast of North Africa. On June 22 Hitler broke the Nazi-Soviet Pact and launched a massive unannounced attack on the USSR, forcing Stalin into the war on the side of the Western allies. Finally, the tension in the Far East came to a head with the Japanese attack on Pearl Harbor. The next day the United States and Britain declared war on Japan. Three days later, December 11, 1941, Germany and Italy declared war on the United States.

A United States poster urges Americans to avenge the Japanese attack on Pearl Harbor. America had a long and strong tradition of neutrality — it had not joined the war on the side of democracy in 1939. However the shock of Pearl Harbor caused America to take action.

WHY HAD IT HAPPENED?

How do we summarize what we have read so far? As with any historical event, we may divide the causes of World War II into long and short term, although the exact boundary between the two is never clear. We may call the long-term causes the preconditions — the conditions prevailing that made war a clear possibility.

Six major preconditions for war may be identified. The first was the flawed settlement at Versailles, which had ended World War I. It is now clear that to blame Germany solely for what had happened in 1914-18 and punish it economically, militarily, and territorially was shortsighted and almost certain to lead to further trouble. The alternatives were either to destroy the country totally, dividing it up between the victors, or, as was done after World War II, help to rebuild a prosperous and confident state that could take its place among the nations of the world.

President Franklin D. Roosevelt asks Congress to declare war on Japan for its "unprovoked and dastardly attack" on Pearl Harbor.

The war against Russia will be such that it cannot be conducted in a knightly fashion. This struggle is one of ideologies and racial differences and will have to be conducted with unprecedented, unmerciful and unrelenting harshness. . . . German soldiers guilty of breaking international law . . . will be excused.

Hitler, discussing his plans for Operation Barbarossa, the invasion of the USSR, 1941.

A second major precondition was the inadequacy of the League of Nations, the official inter-war peace keeper. Its most glaring flaws were the lack of means to enforce its decisions and the absence from its Assembly of major nations, such as the U.S. and, for much of the time, Germany and the USSR.

The worldwide economic slump that began in 1929 must rank as another important long-term cause of war. It played a major part in bringing down unstable democratic governments, such as that in Germany, kept countries like Britain and France short of funds with which to rearm, and set a climate of misery in which extreme political creeds (notably Fascism) were bound to flourish.

The popularity of militaristic philosophies, our fourth precondition, led to the buildup of armaments and aggression. It also brought extremist leaders to prominence: General Hideki Tojo in Japan, Mussolini in Italy and, most importantly, Hitler in Germany. It is generally agreed that Hitler was the individual most responsible for the outbreak of war. Many would argue, however, that there is no point in *blaming* him for what happened, as he achieved what he did only because the circumstances — and other individuals — permitted it. Hitler was as much a *symptom* of inter-war problems as a *cause*.

The last two preconditions are appeasement and the isolationism of the U.S. Although appeasement may be defended on the grounds that it bought time for the democratic states to rearm, it was also responsible for allowing aggressors to grow strong and confident. If, for example, Hitler had been met with armed force when he reoccupied the Rhineland in 1936 (we now know that he had ordered his men to retreat if they met any resistance), the chain of subsequent events would have been very different. Finally, if the United States, the most powerful nation on earth and the most vigorous defender of democracy, had played its full part in the community of nations during the inter-war years, then the League of Nations might have been more effective and aggression nipped in the bud.

The short-term causes, or triggers, of the war are more numerous and more various. They include a series of crucial decisions, such as that of the League not to intervene decisively over Manchuria (1931), Abyssinia (1935), or the reoccupation of the Rhineland (1936). The Munich conference (1938) and Nazi-Soviet Pact (1939) are two other vital milestones on the road to war. Of course, specific dramatic actions were vital. For example, there would have been no war, or it would have been a very different one, had there been no attacks on Poland, the Soviet Union, or Pearl Harbor. And remember that the nature of events was always influenced by chance, as happened during the Marco Polo Bridge incident in China (1937).

Hitler should have understood that Chamberlain's . . . guarantee to Poland was different from anything Britain had so far undertaken. It was public . . . a promise on which even the British would find it difficult to rat.
He [Hitler] had launched the wrong war. And he had done so at the wrong time.

From Ronald Lewin, Hitler's Mistakes, *1984.*

A mobile recruitment station on Fifth Avenue, New York City, attracts passersby for civilian war jobs. When the U.S. finally entered the war in December 1941, its massive industrial and manpower resources made an eventual Allied victory almost inevitable.

YEARS OF WAR

FROM BLITZKRIEG TO STALINGRAD

Unlike World War I, which in the autumn of 1914 many people believed would be "over by Christmas," everyone expected World War II to last a very long time. And it did.

For two and a half years, apart from the continuing conflict in China, the war was largely confined to Europe and North Africa. And it went very much the way of the Axis powers. Having carved up Eastern

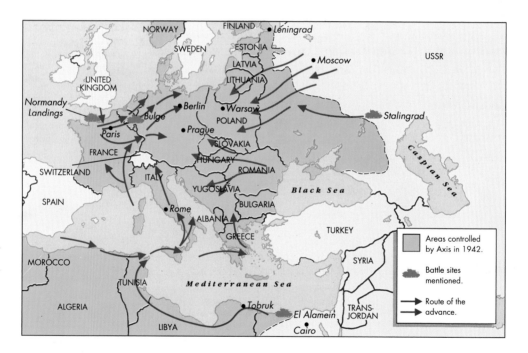

This map shows the main areas of Allied advance in Europe and North Africa during World War II.

Europe with the USSR in 1939, the following year the Germans swept through Western Europe. They began with Scandinavia in April, turning in May to the Low Countries, Luxembourg, and France. Their *Blitzkrieg* (Lightning War) strategy of fierce, rapid attacks of armor and aircraft brought remarkable success, and by the end of June 1940 the conflict was almost over.

The British had been driven back across the English Channel, France was divided, and most other major European states were either under Fascist rule or dominated by the Axis' allies. Spain, Portugal, Switzerland, and Sweden remained neutral.

Over the next few months Britain managed to stem the tide with success in the air battle known as the Battle of Britain. This gave the British air supremacy in the skies over Britain and made an invasion of the island nation impossible. There were also victories over the Italians in Africa. However, in June 1941 German troops successfully launched a dazzling attack on the Soviet Union — Operation Barbarossa. By December the Germans had driven deep into Soviet territory, extending their front line from Leningrad in the north to Sebastopol in the south.

By then, however, something else had happened that would eventually change the war in the Allies' favor. The Japanese attacked the American fleet at Pearl Harbor on December 7, 1941, and the U.S. declared war, first on Japan, and then on Japan's allies in Europe. No country had more resources of people and raw materials to throw into the war effort than the U.S., and the tide rapidly began to turn.

The recapture of the Pacific involved "island-hopping," recapturing one island after the other. This was a very expensive strategy, costing many thousands of Allied lives.

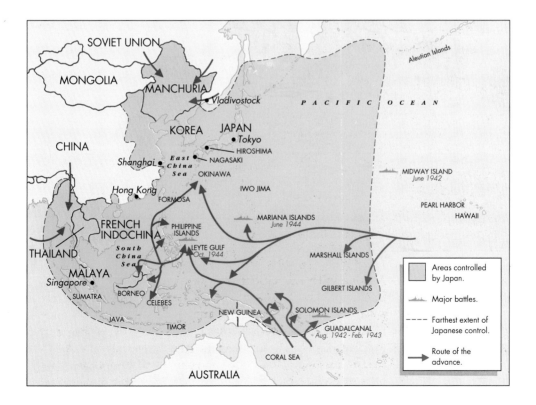

THE TIDE TURNS

Though 1942 was a year of switching fortunes, by the spring of 1943 it was becoming clear that, barring some unforeseen disaster, the combined might of the Allies would eventually triumph. Their armed forces numbered almost twice as many as the Axis powers and they had vastly greater resources, particularly of oil.

Military success was built around these advantages. In May and June 1942 the Americans halted the Japanese advance through the Pacific with decisive air-naval victories at Coral Sea and Midway Island. Later that summer began the crucial offensive against the Japanese on the island of Guadalcanal, a battle that continued well into 1943. In January 1944, the Allies invaded the Marshall Islands and in June, the first B-29s began bombing mainland Japan.

After suffering their first major reverse at El Alamein in North Africa (November 1942), over the following winter the Germans were crushed before the Russian city of Stalingrad. After these battles, victory was largely a matter of grinding the enemy down, and slowly, carefully, and painstakingly winning back the territory that had been lost during the first years of the war. Italy was invaded in 1943, the Philippines in 1944. In the summer of 1944 the largest military invasion in history took place. On D-Day, June 6, Operation Overlord set out to liberate France and the rest of occupied Europe.

Despite setbacks, such as the Battle of the Bulge of December 1944, a massive counterattack by the Germans in Belgium, Allied victory now seemed assured. By spring of the following year, Allied armies were closing on Berlin, and the Americans, with a ferocious struggle, were taking the island of Okinawa, the gateway to mainland Japan. The end was now in sight.

THE UNEASY ALLIES

Long before this, however, the Allied leaders had been turning their minds to the shape of the postwar world. Because Allied victory could be predicted long before it came, there was every reason to begin talking about the final settlement, in the hope of ironing out difficulties and disagreements in advance of the end of hostilities. Everyone was very aware of how the peacemakers' mistakes of 1919-20 had led, almost directly, to the out-

The red flag of the USSR waves over Stalingrad, proclaiming the Germans' failure to take the city. A key point on the Volga River, the city was under attack from August 19, 1942, until the Germans under General Friedrich Paulus finally surrendered on January 30, 1943. The defeat was one of the vital turning points of the war.

break of World War II. No one wanted history to repeat itself. However, the Allies were a poorly-suited group of nations held together only by a common desire to win the war. In particular, the U.S., with its system of free enterprise, and the Communist USSR, with its state–owned system of government, were in conflict with each other before the outbreak of war.

This conflict meant that each of the Allies had rather different war aims. Stalin wanted to create a world safe for the Communist USSR. His country had been invaded during both world wars and had suffered terrible losses. He did not trust the British or the Americans, who he believed had deliberately kept him short of aid and delayed their invasion of France in order to weaken him. Germany had to be totally crushed, and, for the protection of the USSR, a ring of small, Soviet-influenced countries established around the western borders of his nation.

These aims went clean against the wishes of Churchill and Roosevelt. Meeting in Newfoundland in August 1941, they declared in an Atlantic Charter that they sought a world of economic and political cooperation, in which aggressors were disarmed and individual nations allowed to choose their own governments. Although Stalin later accepted the Charter, which became the basis of the United Nations, he mistrusted the ideas of economic cooperation and national self-determination. They were, he felt, merely the West's way of undermining Communism and depriving him of his defensive ring of like-minded states. He was afraid that once the West had

In an alliance the allies should not deceive each other. Perhaps that is naive? Experienced diplomatists may say, "Why should I not deceive my ally?" But I as a naive man think it best not to deceive my ally even if he is a fool. Possibly our alliance is so firm just because we do not deceive each other; or is it because it is not so easy to deceive each other? I propose a toast to the firmness of our Three-Power Alliance. May it be strong and stable; may we be as frank as possible.

From a speech of Stalin's at the Yalta Conference, quoted by Winston Churchill in Triumph and Tragedy, *1951.*

defeated Fascism, it would turn on Communism. For its part, the West was terrified that aggressive, Soviet-inspired Communism would spread through an impoverished postwar world like the plague. Each side feared the other almost as much as it had the enemy.

FROM TEHRAN TO NAGASAKI

The Allied leaders held three major wartime conferences. Stalin, Roosevelt, and Churchill (known popularly as the "Big Three") met at Tehran, Iran, in 1943 and Yalta, in the USSR, in February 1945. Stalin, Harry Truman (in place of Roosevelt, who had died), and Churchill (replaced by Clement Attlee after July 24 when the British general election results were declared) met at Potsdam, Germany, in July-August 1945.

At Tehran the leaders discussed the idea of a United Nations Organization (UN) and agreed to coordinate offensives against Germany the following year. Stalin raised the question of the USSR's future sphere of influence. In some ways the Yalta Conference was more productive, although it highlighted the Allies' differences more clearly. A UN was to be set up. Germany was to pay reparations, particularly to the USSR. It was also proposed that Germany and its capital, Berlin, should be divided into four zones of occupation, to be policed by the USSR, the U.S., Britain, and France. After Germany's surrender, the USSR would join the war against Japan, for which it would receive territorial concessions. Churchill and Stalin informally agreed on a Soviet sphere of influence, to include Bulgaria, Romania, and Hungary. Roosevelt did not want this made official. Although the leaders agreed that free elections should be held in the liberated countries of Eastern Europe, no one said exactly what a free election was.

By the time of the Potsdam Conference Germany had surrendered. Japan, though on the point of defeat, rejected the Allied terms of unconditional surrender suggested during the Potsdam Conference, vowing to "prosecute the war to the bitter end."

Tension was mounting between the Allies. The understanding reached between Churchill and Stalin at Yalta had been overtaken by events: Soviet troops had advanced so fast that they now had armies all over Eastern Europe, including Poland, Czechoslovakia, Austria, and Germany. As many had feared, the new world order seemed on the verge of being as divided as the old.

There was another frightening development. At Potsdam President Truman told Stalin that the U.S. had developed "a new weapon of unusual destructive force." At the time the Soviet leader did not show much interest. He did not realize that Truman's "new weapon" made all others insignificant. It was the atomic bomb. The first one used in anger, nicknamed "Little Boy," was dropped by the B-29 Superfortress *Enola Gay* on the Japanese city of Hiroshima on August 6, 1945, immediately killing between 75,000 and 100,000 people. Hiroshima was destroyed. Three days later Nagasaki was also devastated. The next day the Japanese emperor announced his country's surrender, avoiding an eventual invasion of Japan.

World War II was at an end. Now the world had to start counting the cost and coming to terms with the consequences of what had happened.

On August 6 came the historic news that shook the world. I was eating lunch with members of the *Augusta's* crew when the watch officer handed me the following message:
To the President
From the Secretary of War
Big bomb dropped on Hiroshima 5 August at 7.15 p.m. Washington time [6 August in Japan]. First reports indicate complete success. I was greatly moved. I telephoned Byrnes [U.S. Secretary of State] aboard ship to give him the news and then said to the group of sailors around me, "This is the greatest thing in history."

From Harry S. Truman, Memoirs, 1955.

The ruins of the Japanese city of Nagasaki after its destruction by the second U.S. atomic bomb, nicknamed "Fat Man," on August 9, 1945. The 10,000-pound bomb was originally intended for the army base at Kokura. At the last minute the target was changed to Nagasaki because of the weather. Up to 80,000 people are estimated to have been killed or wounded, including many who died later from the effects of radiation.

39

DESTRUCTION AND SUFFERING

THE AFTERMATH IN EUROPE

Life must go on — survivors wander amid the ruins of the bombed Soviet city of Murmansk in the far north, 1942. Only the stone chimneys remain of the buildings that were once there. The port was of strategic importance, the destination of supply convoys carrying goods from Britain. British losses on the Arctic route were so great that convoys were twice suspended.

The most immediate and obvious consequences of World War II were massive destruction and loss of life. Partly because of the number of countries involved and partly because of the effectiveness of modern weapons, these were on a far greater scale than in any previous war. Perhaps the most striking and ghastly aspect was the havoc wrought on civilians. In the past, of course, noncombatants had suffered in war, but never on such a scale.

The loss was greatest in the USSR. We can, in fact, make sense of the postwar world only if we recall what that country went through. A comparison with the U.S. makes the point most clearly.

Throughout the war no enemy army set foot on the United States. The economy boomed under the impetus of wartime requirements. The gross national product and industrial output doubled. The war cost America a few civilians and 405,000 servicemen.

The precise figures for Soviet casualties are not known. It is suggested, however, that the country lost at least 20 million people. On top of that, 28 million Soviets were left homeless. In the west of the country three quarters of all houses in the countryside had been destroyed. Two-thirds of all wealth disappeared. For mile after mile there were no houses, no roads, no bridges, no telegraph poles. Most of the livestock were dead. Industry and communications were in ruins. This, then, was the unspeakable desolation which lay behind so much of Soviet thinking after 1945. Whatever the cost, Soviet leaders were determined never to be invaded again.

Germany lost three and a half million soldiers (twice the number of World War I) and one million civilians. Many of its cities had been gutted by Allied bombing. After the war the country was forcibly divided and, particularly in the east, stripped of many remaining industrial plants by the victors. The Japanese, although fighting on a very broad front, lost about two million. Chinese losses are impossible to ascertain. Estimates vary from 2.5 million to 13.5 million of both soldiers and civilians.

Over the rest of Europe there were shattered cities, broken communications, abandoned fields, and drifting, helpless refugees. The raw casualty figures sometimes disguise the nature of what had happened. The 200,000 Dutch civilian deaths, for example, represent the highest figure in relation to the size of population outside Germany. Britain lost 450,000, France slightly more, and Italy slightly less. Two-thirds of all Greek losses were civilians. The total of men, women, and children killed during the war may have been about 50 million. The number of wounded, in body, mind, or spirit, cannot be counted.

There is one glaring omission from the figures so far mentioned. A major part of the Nazi philosophy was the purity of the Aryan (white, Anglo-Saxon) race and the inferiority of all other races. In 1939 the Nazi authorities began a "euthanasia program" for their own country's mentally ill. It claimed 90,000 lives. Later, as the German armies swept east, bringing mil-

Emaciated survivors of one of the largest Nazi concentration camps, at Evensee, Austria. These men were liberated by the 80th Division, U.S. Third Army on May 4, 1945.

lions of citizens under the Reich's control, the Nazis
began the systematic elimination of all groups they
considered undesirable. These included homosexuals,
priests, Communists, gypsies, the Polish ruling classes, and, above all, the Jews. At a conference held at
Wannsee in January 1942, a decision was taken to
implement the "final solution" to the "Jewish problem." The entire race of European Jews was to be
wiped out. As a result, in what is known as the
Holocaust, almost six million Jews were gassed, shot,
or died of neglect or ill-treatment.

WAR CRIMES ON TRIAL

As a result of the inhumane behavior of some Axis
leaders a series of "war crimes" tribunals were established shortly after the end of the war. Although several former Axis leaders, including Hitler himself,
preferred suicide to the humiliation of capture and
trial, many others were rounded up. Investigation into

*A cartoon illustrates how the
Soviets thought
the legal process
at the Nuremberg
trials was allowing Nazi criminals to escape
justice. The
International
Military Tribunal
met in Nuremberg
from November
1945 to September
1946 to put war
criminals on trial.*

the behavior of 177 German and Austrian Nazis began at Nuremberg in 1945. In 13 separate trials, 25 were sentenced to death and 20 given life imprisonment; 97 were given shorter sentences, 35 were acquitted. Similar processes were held in Tokyo, Hong Kong, Singapore, Borneo, and other places that had suffered Japanese occupation. The Tokyo court sentenced seven to death. Elsewhere over 900 "war criminals" were executed. Some people claimed these trials were not legal, but no one could suggest another method of punishment for these inhumane crimes.

A JEWISH HOMELAND

One important consequence of the Holocaust was the hastening of the formation of the state of Israel, a focus of major conflict and tension in the postwar world. Between the wars Britain had been responsible for looking after Palestine, the state at the eastern end of the Mediterranean inhabited by Jews and Arabs, and had unwisely promised both races that they would be the eventual rulers of the region. Even before the war large numbers of European Jews had sought sanctuary in Palestine. As news of the Holocaust spread, worldwide sympathy for the Jews increased. At the same time, Jewish nationalists launched a fierce campaign for large areas of Palestine to become Israel — the Jewish homeland. This was agreed to by the United Nations in 1948, and the area was divided into a Jewish state and an Arab state.

The Arab nations refused to accept this decision. On the day following Israel's proclamation of independence on May 14, 1948, the country was invaded by several Arab armies. The attack was unsuccessful and Israelis seized all but one of the territories the UN had allocated to the Palestinian Arabs. Fighting broke out again in 1955, and there were full-scale Arab-Israeli wars in 1967 and 1973. These were made all the more dangerous because of "superpower" involvement (see page 59). Broadly speaking, the U.S. backed Israel, while the Arab nations — particularly Egypt and Syria — were supported by the USSR. The Camp David agreement of 1978 ended the hostilities between Egypt and Israel, but did not solve the overall Middle East problem. Fighting between Palestinians and Israelis, particularly in Lebanon, continued into the 1990s, although peace efforts had some effect in 1994.

The Land of Israel was the birthplace of the Jewish people. Here their spiritual, religious and national identity was formed. Here they achieved independence and created a culture of national and universal significance. . . . The recent holocaust, which engulfed millions of Jews in Europe, proved anew the need to solve the problem of the homelessness and lack of independence of the Jewish people by means of the re-establishment of the Jewish state. . . . On November 29, 1947, the General Assembly of the United Nations adopted a Resolution requiring the establishment of a Jewish State in Palestine. . . . ACCORDINGLY WE, the members of the National Council, . . . HEREBY PROCLAIM the establishment of the Jewish State in Palestine, to be called Medinath Yisrael (The State of Israel).

Israel's Proclamation of Independence, Tel Aviv, May 14, 1948

AN IRON CURTAIN

THE SPREAD OF COMMUNISM

Compared with the re-drawing of Europe that took place in 1919-20, there was comparatively little realignment of national frontiers after World War II. What did happen, though, was a re-drawing of boundaries according to political ideology.

In 1945 the USSR took over Karelia from Finland, Bessarabia from Romania, Ruthenia from Czechoslovakia, and northeast Prussia from Germany. It also acquired part of eastern Poland and the formerly independent countries of Latvia, Lithuania, and Estonia. Short of starting another war, which was almost unthinkable, no one could stop this happening because the Red Army was already in possession of these territories.

Having thus created the first part of his buffer against invasion by expanding the USSR eastward, Stalin then proceeded to make sure he was surrounded by states favorable to Communism. First came Poland. At Yalta it had been agreed that the provisional government of the pro-Communist Lubin group could remain in power until "free and fair" elections could be held. These were never called, and Poland remained under the thumb of the Soviets until 1989.

Stalin made it quite clear at Yalta that he wished to see a "complete disarmament, demilitarization and dismemberment" of Germany. Since the Red Army had been the first Allied force to invade the homeland of the Third Reich, it was comparatively easy for him to see that this happened. The Soviets milked every available resource from the large zone of eastern Germany under their control, and in 1949 they arranged for the territory to become a separate Communist state under Soviet domination — the German Democratic Republic. In the same year the rest of the country, comprising the areas occupied by the United States, France, and Britain, became the Federal Republic of Germany. A divided Germany,

Two leaders of the Hungarian uprising stand with the Hungarian national flag in Budapest in November 1956. The revolt was quickly suppressed and its perpetrators were hunted down and killed.

Stalin believed, would never again be strong enough to threaten the USSR. The two halves of the country were finally reunited on October 3, 1990, 37 years after Stalin's death.

Hungary was treated equally ruthlessly. As a former ally of Nazi Germany, it was invaded toward the end of the war by Russian and Romanian troops and came under Soviet control. In addition to losing two-thirds of its national wealth in the war, the country had to pay heavy reparations to the USSR and was obliged to become a "Republic of Workers and Working Peasants" under a Soviet-approved government. A revolt against Communist domination was ruthlessly crushed by Soviet tanks in 1956 and the country had to wait until 1990 before free elections were held.

Stalin's Communist frontier was not yet complete. Bulgaria, another of Hitler's allies, was added in 1946, when the monarchy was abolished and the country put under a Communist administration. At the beginning of the war Romania had been on the side of the Axis powers, and it declared war on the USSR in 1941. Then, in 1944, King Michael managed to overthrow the government and side his country with the Allies. He did not last long, however, for in 1946 a Soviet-backed Communist administration came

to power and forced him to abdicate. The next year
Romania became the Romanian People's Republic, controlled by the Communist Party.

Czechoslovakia was outside the Soviet bloc until
1948, when a Communist-dominated government held
elections in which no opposition parties were permitted to run. From then until 1989, with a brief inter-
lude in 1968 known as the "Prague Spring,"
Czechoslovakia remained firmly under Soviet influence. That Yugoslavia did not go the same way was
largely due to Marshal Tito, the leader of the guerril-
las who had fought against the German invaders.
Although Communist and initially supported by the
Soviet Union, Tito's government soon made it clear
that it was not going to be told what to do by Moscow.
In 1948 Stalin expelled the Yugoslavian Communist
Party from the "family of Fraternal Communist
Parties" and the country remained nonaligned until its
fearful disintegration in the 1990s. Greek democracy
was propped up by massive Western aid, and Austria
remained partitioned until 1955, when it became an
independent country, promising to remain neutral.
With the unimportant exception of Albania, which
went Communist in 1946, the rest of Europe returned,
more or less, to the form of government that had pre-
vailed before the rise of Fascism. Italy lost
some territory to Yugoslavia. The Italian overseas
empire was also lost.

THE COLD WAR

It was Winston Churchill who summed up most accurately what was happening. Speaking at Fulton, Missouri, in March 1946, he said: "From Stettin in the Baltic, to Trieste, in the Adriatic, an iron curtain has descended across the continent. Behind that curtain . . . all are subject to Soviet influence and a very high degree of control from Moscow." This speech is generally said to mark the beginning of what is called the "Cold War" between East and West. It is called a "cold" war because there was no direct fighting between the Communist USSR and the democratic U.S. — a shooting war would have been a "hot" war. Today it is often suggested that the Cold War was an unnecessary confrontation, arising more out of fear and misunderstanding than hostility. The West believed that the elections which had allowed Communist governments to come to power in Eastern Europe were rigged. The Soviets said that they merely reflected the will of the people. America was afraid that the USSR was trying to make the whole world Communist. The Soviets believed the West was engaged in a crusade against Communism. As we have seen, Stalin was determined to protect his country's frontiers at all costs. Since August 1945 he had a new fear, too — American possession of the atomic bomb. Soviet scientists were instructed to come up with their own bomb as soon as possible. The Americans responded by making bigger and more powerful bombs and finding new ways of delivering them. As if the Cold War were not enough, there was soon an arms race as well.

America's first response to what it saw as the advance of Communism was the Truman Doctrine. In a speech to Congress in March 1947, President Truman declared, "I believe that it must be the policy of the United States to support free peoples who are resisting

Cold War propaganda — a Soviet poster shows how the Russians feared American aggression, with U.S. troops firing nerve gas. Although both sides lost no opportunity to criticize each other, fear of an atomic holocaust prevented the East-West Cold War from developing into an all-out military conflict.

subjugation by armed minorities or by outside pressures." Two points are worth thinking about in this remark. Firstly, it marks a completely different approach to foreign policy from that shown by the U.S. government in 1919, when they had withdrawn from the world scene almost as soon as the war had finished. Now they were setting themselves up as the protectors of democratic capitalism. Secondly, Truman does not mention Communism or the USSR by name. But there was no mistaking whom, and what he was talking about. American armed forces remained in Western Europe, and before long there was American money, too.

In April 1947 Congress accepted the Truman Doctrine. The following month it voted $250 million in aid for Turkey and Greece, to help them against the threat of Communism. The next year Marshall Aid, named after Secretary of State George Marshall, went into operation. This was massive funding for all European democracies to help them recover from the war. A prosperous Western Europe, Marshall reasoned, was unlikely to be attracted to Communism. It would also act as a buffer between the USSR and the U.S. and make a good trading partner. From 1948 to 1952, $13 billion came to Europe in Marshall Aid, Britain, France, and West Germany receiving most of it.

Funds from the Marshall Plan are here used by Berliners to construct a new apartment house in an area of the city destroyed by Allied bombardment.

An aircraft beats the blockade of Berlin after the Russians closed land routes into the city through East Germany in 1948. During the crisis aircraft kept the Western sector of the city supplied with food and other necessities until the roads were reopened in May 1949.

THE BERLIN CRISIS

By the beginning of 1948 it was clear that East and West had totally different plans for Germany. The country was still divided into its four zones of occupation, with Berlin inside the Russian zone but also split between French, British, Soviet, and U.S. administrations. West Berlin was in a highly vulnerable position. This became evident in June 1948 when, in protest over plans for the economic reorganization of the Western zones, the Soviets imposed a total land blockade on that part of the city. With no supplies from Western Europe arriving by road or rail, the whole of Berlin seemed doomed to fall into Communist hands.

The Anglo-American response was not to risk war by forcing a passage to the beleaguered city through the Soviet zone, but to supply the city by air. The Berlin airlift lasted until 1949. By then it was clear that the West was not prepared to let the city go and the blockade was lifted. It was also clear by this time that the Cold War was not just a temporary phenomenon, but a lasting feature of the postwar world. To confirm this, Belgium, France, Luxembourg, the Netherlands, Britain, the U.S., Canada, Denmark, Iceland, Italy, Norway, and Portugal came together to form a military alliance, the North Atlantic Treaty Organization, or NATO. By its terms, all member countries agreed to go to the aid of one of their number if it was attacked.

When Berlin falls, Western Germany will be next. If we withdraw our position in Berlin, Europe is threatened . . . Communism will run rampant.

General Lucius Clay, the U.S. commander in Berlin, 1948, cited in Peter Fisher, The Great Power Conflict After 1945, *1985.*

49

THE WORLD OF THE SUPERPOWERS

A NEW WORLD ORDER

The postwar map of Europe was very different from that in 1939. The Eastern bloc of states dominated by the Soviet Union was separated by an "iron curtain" from the democratic nations of the West.

During the interwar years, as for much of modern history, a number of countries had been regarded as great powers. A combination of features made a state a great power. These included a large land area and population, plentiful natural resources, a stable political system, wealth, and substantial armed forces. By these criteria, the United States, France, Germany, Britain, and the USSR were all undoubtedly great powers, with Italy, Japan, and China perhaps in the second rank. As

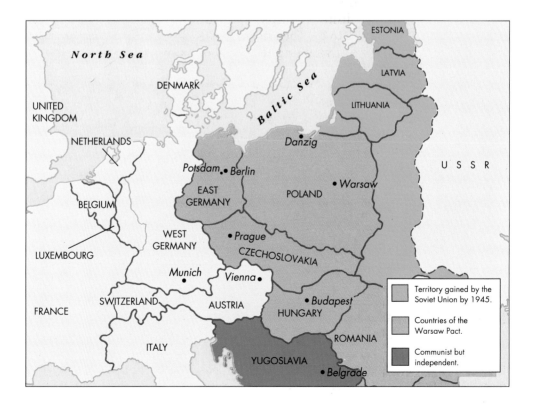

a result of World War II, however, the list was cut to two — the U.S. and the USSR, for whom we use the term superpowers. How had this happened?

Defeat in war and harsh peace terms had destroyed Germany, Italy, and Japan as world powers. China was convulsed in civil war. France had been crippled by occupation. Britain was at the end of an era, although it took the British some time to realize this. As a small island with few plentiful natural resources, and a population only a fraction that of the U.S., the USSR, or China, Britain's worldwide power had been an historical phenomenon of the later-eighteenth and nineteenth centuries. It was based on commerce, a powerful navy, the possession of a huge overseas empire, and the fact that the country had been the first to undergo an industrial revolution, which for a time gave it an enormous advantage over its trading competitors.

By the 1930s, however, the brief years of glory were over. Other countries had overtaken Britain in industrial output and the country was finding it increasingly difficult to hold its empire together. World War II was the final push that removed Britain's great power status. The main problem was economic. The war cost billions of dollars, much of it paid to the U.S. for vital weapons, machinery, ships, and so forth, which Britain was unable to produce itself. By 1946-50 the balance of trade was averaging a deficit of more than $200 million annually.

With the emergence of a world dominated by two superpowers, all nations needed to decide whether they were in the U.S. or Soviet spheres of influence, or chose to remain nonaligned. As we have seen, most Arab countries were in the Soviet circle, because the U.S. protected Israel. This presented problems for states such as Saudi Arabia, whose conservative monarchy was the very opposite of Communism. China, the nations of Eastern Europe, and some of the newly independent nations also looked to the USSR for economic and ideological support. Other nations, such as India, Yugoslavia, and Indonesia formed the center of an influential band of nonaligned countries.

THE KOREAN WAR

The Berlin blockade was only the first of several trials of strength between the superpowers. The Soviet Union exploded its first atomic bomb in 1949, making the U.S. even more concerned about what it saw as the Communist threat. Then, on June 25, 1950, an event occurred which the U.S. government believed proved all its fears correct. Communist North Korea, backed by the USSR, attacked South Korea, whose government was dependent upon the U.S. The next day the Security Council of the United Nations ordered the North Koreans to withdraw. When they refused, the UN called on a multinational force to drive them out. The U.S., who provided most of the men and munitions, was very willing to oblige. Thus began the first open superpower conflict.

At first the North Koreans were successful, driving deep into South Korea. Then, as the might of the U.S. made itself felt, the UN drove their enemy back to the frontier with China, by then a Communist country. (North Korea has a boundary with both the USSR and China.) At this point, hundreds of thousands of Chinese troops entered the conflict and the UN was driven back to the 38th parallel, the original (and present) dividing line between North and South Korea. With the battle almost at a stalemate, an armistice was signed on July 17, 1953. No one had won, although the Americans claimed to have held

An American soldier patrols the streets of Inchon, Korea, in 1950. The Korean War began as a United Nations response to South Korea's plea for help against an invasion by Communist North Korea. The conflict very nearly ended in all-out war between the U.S. and China.

The Cold War commanders, John F. Kennedy and Nikita Khrushchev, met in Vienna in 1961. Despite the friendly handshake, relations between the two were not amicable, and were fraught with the tension of several major crises — an abortive attempt to invade Cuba, which was backed by Kennedy, the Cuban missile crisis, and the building of the Berlin Wall.

back the Communist tide. More significant for the future, perhaps, was the ability of China to challenge the might of the U.S. A new superpower was in the making.

Shortly before the end of the Korean War, the U.S. announced a new and even more devastating weapon — the hydrogen bomb. The version tested was more powerful than the total of all bombs dropped by both sides in the whole of World War II. Its radioactive fallout was far greater than that of an atomic bomb. Within a year the USSR had developed an H-bomb of its own.

With the death of Stalin in 1953, leadership of the USSR passed to Chairman Nikita Khrushchev and the Cold War eased a little. For the first time since 1945, East and West met in high-level talks to try to lessen the threat of a long-range missile war. Nevertheless, the tensions continued. The brutality with which the Soviets suppressed uprisings in the Eastern Bloc countries (East Germany 1953 and Hungary 1956) horrified the West. In 1955, under Soviet leadership, the Iron Curtain countries formed the Warsaw Pact to counterbalance NATO. Two years later the U.S. was shocked to hear that the USSR had launched the world's first orbiting satellite, *Sputnik*. This implied that the Soviets were ahead in the "space race" and therefore

You are worried over Cuba. You say that it worries you because it lies at a distance of 90 miles across the sea from the shores of the United States. However, Turkey [where the U.S. had rocket bases] lies next to us. Our sentinels are pacing up and down and watching each other. Do you believe that you have the right to demand security for your country, and the removal of such weapons that you qualify as offensive, while not recognizing the right for us?

Chairman Nikita Khrushchev in a letter to President Kennedy, October 1962.

The Soviet Union stole a march on the United States by launching the earliest artificial satellites. The first went into space in October 1957. Sputnik II, shown here, was launched in November 1957 with a dog as passenger.

might soon be in a position to attack the U.S. with nuclear weapons from beyond the Earth's atmosphere. This fear increased when the Soviets put a man in space in 1961. It was one of the main reasons for this statement, made by President John F. Kennedy in May 1961: "I believe this nation should commit itself to achieving the goal, before this decade is out, of landing a man on the moon and returning him safely to earth." The goal was achieved, but Kennedy would not live to see his dream fulfilled.

THE CUBAN CRISIS

I have read your letter . . . with great care and welcomed the statement of your desire to seek a prompt solution to the problem. The first thing that needs to be done, however, is for work to cease on offensive missile bases in Cuba and for all weapons systems in Cuba capable of offensive use to be rendered inoperable . . . .

President Kennedy's reply to Chairman Khrushchev, October 1962.

With the construction of a massive wall between East and West Berlin in 1961, the Cold War entered its most dangerous phase. In 1962 President Kennedy told the Soviets that if they did not remove their missile sites from the island of Cuba, off the Florida coast, he was prepared to go to war to remove them himself. For a few hours the massed forces of the superpowers were on red alert. Missiles stood targeted on their launch pads. Huge airplanes, their bellies laden with live nuclear weapons, were in the air waiting for the signal to attack. In Germany soldiers prepared for war. In the end, however, the Soviets relented and agreed to dismantle the Cuban bases. A special "hot line" was set up between Moscow and Washington so that the leaders of the Communist and capitalist blocs could speak directly to each other in moments of crisis. Gradually, from this time forward, the threat of an East–West war receded. Just, and only just, the worst possible consequence of World War II had been avoided.

END OF THE COLD WAR

The Cold War was undoubtedly the most dangerous legacy of World War II. Sometimes thawing and sometimes heating up almost to a third world war, it continued for 40 years. Only when Mikhail Gorbachev became First Secretary of the Communist Party of the USSR in 1985 and the Soviet system began its spectacular collapse, did the decades of fear and mistrust come to an end.

The most powerful symbol of the Cold War was the Berlin Wall, constructed by the Communists in 1961 to stop the stream of refugees from the Eastern sector of the city leaving for the freer and more prosperous West. By the end of 1989 the Communist Party in East Germany was on the verge of collapse, a process set in motion by President Gorbachev's reforms in the Soviet Union. In November crowds gathered to participate in the momentous tearing down of the Wall.

THE
UNITED NATIONS

United Nations mediators on the disputed frontier between India and Pakistan in 1955. The presence of such neutral forces frequently helps to deter aggression and encourages the settlement of differences through negotiation.

Humans have long dreamed of the whole world living in harmony. As we have seen, after World War I a League of Nations was set up in an attempt to bring this about. The League was specifically intended to maintain world peace, encourage a reduction in armaments, improve conditions of life worldwide, and protect states from aggression. In its humanitarian work the League of Nations had a number of successes, but, unfortunately, as a peacekeeper it proved to be a dismal failure. During World War II, therefore, politicians started to consider the idea of a new international organization to replace the League. The result was the United Nations.

Following the Arab-Israeli war of 1948-49, the United Nations faced a massive task finding shelter for Palestinian refugees. Four years later the 6,000 refugees in this camp near Tripoli in Lebanon were still living in tents, which provided little protection either from the heat in summer or the rain and cold of winter. Eventually the tents were replaced with concrete huts.

The UN emerged out of a meeting of 50 nations in San Francisco in the spring of 1945. Its charter was drawn up the following October. The new organization's three purposes were to maintain world peace, develop friendly relations between nations, and promote international efforts at economic, cultural, and social justice. The UN's principal body is the General Assembly, in which each national member has a voice and a vote. Answering to the Assembly are the Trusteeship Council, which supervises territory administered by the UN; the International Court of Justice at The Hague, the Netherlands; the Economic and Social Council; the Secretariat, headed by the Secretary-General; and the Security Council. The UN has its headquarters in New York City.

In the immediate aftermath of World War II, the UN's principal function was peacekeeping. Responsibility for this rested with the Security Council (comprising five permanent members — the U.S., the USSR, China, Britain, and France — and six, later ten, other members elected for two years each) and the Secretary-General. To overcome the difficulties faced by the League, the Council was empowered not only to arrange cease-fires and impose sanctions, but also to intervene in disputes with force when necessary. To avoid unpopular decisions, the five permanent members were given a veto over all resolutions.

If the postwar world had not been divided between the two superpowers, the UN might have been able to do what was expected of it. As it was, the Security Council veto made it almost impossible to get agree-

We, the peoples of the United Nations, determined to save succeeding generations from the scourge of war, which twice in our lifetime has brought untold sorrow to mankind, and to reaffirm faith in fundamental human rights . . . and to promote social progress . . . do hereby establish an international organization to be known as the United Nations.

From the Charter of the United Nations, 1945

ment to act decisively. Since much of the world was in either the Soviet or the American spheres of influence, one or the other was bound to object whenever it was suggested that the UN might intervene actively in a dispute. The one exception was Korea. However, the armed intervention of the UN in this conflict was more the result of a technical hitch than a universal agreement. At the time two administrations claimed to be the legitimate government of China. One was the Communist government in Peking, which controlled all mainland China, the other was the exiled Nationalist government on the island of Formosa (now Taiwan), which had held nominal power over the whole of China until defeated in the civil war and driven out. (See page 60.) At American insistence, the Nationalists held China's permanent place on the Security Council. In protest at this bizarre decision, the USSR walked out. It was during the Soviet absence that the vote to go to the aid of South Korea was taken. The Soviet delegation soon realized their mistake, and the Council passed no further resolution for UN armed intervention until the Cold War had ended.

The United Nations headquarters in New York. While siting the building in a Western capital was not a politically neutral gesture, it is unlikely that any other country could have afforded to host the organization.

The best example of a confrontation in which the superpower hostility prevented the UN from acting effectively was the Arab-Israeli dispute. In 1947 the General Assembly proposed partitioning Palestine between Jews and Arabs. The Israelis, with U.S. backing, prevented this from happening. The UN arranged the truce which ended the 1948-49 war, but it had been unable to stop the fighting. In 1956, when Britain, France, and Israel invaded Egypt and seized the Suez Canal, in the Six-Day War of 1967, and in the Yom Kippur War of 1973, the UN was able to do no more than call for cease-fires and send observers between the front lines when the fighting had stopped.

In the light of this, however, it would be wrong to think that the UN has been as ineffective as the old League of Nations. The balance of fear between the USSR and the U.S. certainly did more to maintain world peace than the efforts of the UN, but the organization had plenty of other successes. The Secretary-General played a key role in keeping communications open between Kennedy and Khrushchev during the Cuban missile crisis of 1962. UN peacekeeping forces helped to promote stability and peace in the divided Cyprus after 1964, in the Belgian Congo (now Zaïre) from 1960 to 1964, and in the disputed region of Kashmir following the separation of India and Pakistan in 1947. Moreover, the UN has supervised arms limitation treaties, worked tirelessly to improve world health, dealt with emergencies such as famine and flood, and promoted human rights everywhere.

Optimists are disappointed that the UN has not achieved everything that it set out to do. Cynics are amazed that it has achieved anything at all. Most people would agree, however, that the UN is undoubtedly one of World War II's more worthy legacies.

An enthusiastic welcome greets United Nations mediators in war-torn Namibia in southwest Africa. Peacekeeping is one of the UN's most difficult and controversial roles.

A NEW ASIA AND A NEW EUROPE

CIVIL WAR IN CHINA

In the Far East the most important consequence of the ending of World War II was a fresh outbreak of the Chinese civil war. Fought between the Communists, led by Mao Zedong, and the Nationalists (GMD), led by Jiang Jieshi, the conflict had lasted, on and off, since the late 1920s. In 1945, once the Japanese were out of the way, it flared up again, despite American efforts to mediate between the two sides. This time it was to be a fight to the finish.

As one might expect, the United States was unwilling to stand by and watch the most populous country in the world fall to Communism. Between 1946 and 1949 they provided the GMD with $6 billion in aid, as well as 1,000 aircraft and other machinery and weaponry. It was all to no avail. The government of Jiang Jieshi was corrupt, inefficient, and ineffective. Furthermore, it bore responsibility for the country's failure to combat the Japanese invasion. Consequently, it was deeply unpopular with the mass of the Chinese people, who flocked to the red banners of the Communists in the millions. The GMD launched a futile offensive, then crumbled. By the autumn of 1949 China had become a Communist state, and the government and the army of the GMD fled to Taiwan.

This remarkable victory was a great blow for American prestige and a relief for the Soviets, who welcomed their new neighbor with an "everlasting and unbreakable" Treaty of Friendship, Alliance and Mutual Assistance (1950). The Communist success inevitably raised the temperature of the Cold War, and was one reason why the U.S. was so eager to prevent further Communist success in Korea and, later, in Vietnam. The U.S. need not have worried, however. Firstly, the Chinese leadership was far too preoccupied with its massive domestic problems, which it aggravated from time to time with lunatic campaigns such as the Great Leap Forward (1958) and the Cultural

Revolution (1966 onward), to play a major part on the international stage. Secondly, the age-old hostility between Russia and China ran too deep for their new friendship to last. In 1960 Soviet aid to China dried up and eleven years later the Americans agreed that China should replace Taiwan on the United Nations Security Council. In 1972 the new Sino-American concord was cemented by a visit to China of President Richard Nixon, the first U. S. President to make such a visit.

THE JAPANESE ECONOMY REBORN

The initial consequences of World War II on Japan were horrific. One quarter of all homes had been destroyed. Most factories were in ruins. Millions were unemployed, thousands were starving, and no one had any money. At the cessation of hostilities Japan was occupied by U.S. troops under the command of General Douglas MacArthur. The troops remained there for many years to maintain law and order and ensure that the new system of government operated in accordance with democratic principles. Remembering the lessons learned from the aftermath of World War I, however, the U.S. also poured money into Japan to get it back on its feet again as soon as possible. $2 billion was given between 1945 and 1951, and a further $4 billion was spent there during the course of the Korean War. Other factors that helped Japanese recovery included the redistribution of land to the peasants and the clause in the country's constitution that prevented it from having any armed forces. This allowed spending, which in other countries went on defense, to be directed toward industry and technology. During the 1950s and 1960s the Japanese economy grew twice as fast as those of other industrial nations. It is one of the great ironies of history that modern Japan, risen from the ashes of war,

An American military policeman helps with traffic control in Tokyo, 1945. The U.S. occupation of Japan lasted until 1952 and was generally benign — both sides treating each other with respect. In 1948 a plan for the economic revival of Japan was adopted which aimed for economic independence within five years. To achieve this the U.S. provided massive amounts of aid.

has far more international power and influence than its prewar, militaristic counterpart.

THE EUROPEAN COMMUNITY

Western Europe also underwent a radical transformation as a result of the war. As farsighted European leaders considered the destruction and suffering around them and noted the way the continent was dominated by the American and Soviet superpowers, they came to two conclusions. To begin with, some means had to be found to ensure that the countries of Europe never went to war with each other again. And secondly, they had to learn to work together if they were to compete successfully with the U.S. and the USSR.

The first step came as a result of the Marshall Plan, which had given aid on condition that Europeans also worked to help themselves. This led to the Organization for European Economic Co-operation (OEEC), founded in 1948 to distribute U.S. assistance. Three years later the European Coal and Steel Community (ECSC) was born, comprising West Germany, France, Italy, Belgium, the Netherlands and Luxembourg. These nations, known as the "Six," did not just agree to cooperate over economic matters, they also set up an independent high authority to supervise common activities. This was the first step toward a European government. The next step was even more

Land, sea and air forces will never be maintained. The Japanese people for ever renounce war as a sovereign right of the nation, and the threat or use of force as a means of settling international disputes.

From Article IX of the Japanese Constitution, 1947.

A Super-Express train passes through Tokyo in 1965. No country recovered from the ravages of World War II more quickly than Japan. Between 1953, shortly after the withdrawal of the last U.S. forces of occupation, and 1965 industrial output grew by an amazing 10 percent a year.

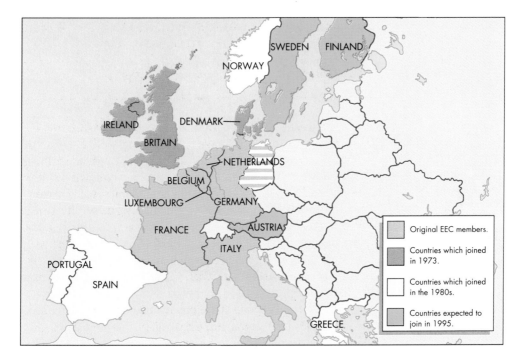

SWEDEN FINLAND
NORWAY
IRELAND
DENMARK—
BRITAIN
NETHERLANDS
BELGIUM
LUXEMBOURG GERMANY
FRANCE AUSTRIA
ITALY
PORTUGAL
SPAIN
GREECE

Original EEC members.

Countries which joined in 1973.

Countries which joined in the 1980s.

Countries expected to join in 1995.

momentous. Meeting in Rome in 1957, the Six formed the European Atomic Energy Commission (Euratom) and the European Economic Community (EEC). In 1967 all three existing European organizations were merged to form the European Community (EC). Since then a succession of additional countries have joined the Community, starting with Britain, Ireland, and Denmark in 1973.

Nothing like the EC had ever been seen before. It consisted of a Council of Ministers from all the member countries, a Commission (civil service), a Court of Justice, and an elected European Parliament. Its aims were to maintain Europe's place in the world and ensure a continuous rise in the living standards of its people. By no means everything that the Community attempted was successful. It had considerable trouble with its agriculture budget, for example, and ran into serious difficulties when trying to coordinate the foreign policies of its various members. Nevertheless, 50 years after Europeans had been tearing each other apart in a bloody war, they were sitting in the same parliament, carrying the same passports, and obeying many of the same laws and regulations. And their Community had become one of the world's biggest trading blocs. It was a remarkable achievement. The only tragedy is that it took a war to make it happen.

This map shows how the European Community (now known as the European Union) has expanded to include almost all of western Europe. Many members of the former Warsaw Pact have been promised membership.

We must build a kind of United States of Europe . . . Time may be short. At present there is breathing space, but if we are to form a United States of Europe — or whatever name it may take — then we must begin now. I say to you: let it arise.

Winston Churchill, speaking in Switzerland in September 1945.

FOR BETTER OR FOR WORSE

A German V2 rocket launch in 1945. The 46-foot long, liquid fueled weapon weighed about a ton, and flew at an altitude of 50 miles. About 5,000 were fired during 1944-1945. They were unreliable, however, and buried themselves too deep in the ground to make the best use of their warheads.

World War II had exploded on a divided world. Paradoxically, although the post-1945 world was, if anything, even more divided politically than the world before the war, it was also in some ways smaller and more united. In the second half of the 20th century human beings learned more about each other and came closer to sharing the same values and culture than ever before. This was partly the result of technological developments and partly a strange and unexpected spin-off from the Cold War.

THE TRIUMPH OF TECHNOLOGY

Like most modern wars, World War II significantly quickened the pace of technological change. Much of what was developed proved a double-edged sword, either helping or hindering humankind depending on how it was employed.

The single most dramatic advance was in learning how to harness the vast quantities of energy harbored in the smallest known particles — atoms. Before the war British scientists had been carrying out research into the possibility of developing an atomic bomb. With the outbreak of hostilities, the top-secret work moved to the United States, where it then became known as the Manhattan Project. Sabotage seriously hampered German efforts to develop a similar weapon.

After years of research and development, including test

detonations, President Harry Truman finally gave permission for the atomic bomb to be used in action. He justified this by saying that, powerful though the atomic bomb was, it would bring the war to a close more swiftly and save more lives both American and Japanese than prolonged conventional warfare. In the event, the virtual obliteration of the centers of Hiroshima and Nagasaki, killing every living thing, was perhaps more horrifying than anyone had foreseen. But by the time the full realization of the new weapon's gigantic power had begun to sink in, it was too late. The genie could not be put back in the bottle.

It was not long before other nations — the USSR, Britain, France, and China — developed their own atomic weapons. Scientists devised vastly more destructive hydrogen and nuclear bombs, which were stockpiled by the thousand around the world. This was without doubt World War II's most terrifying legacy. Human beings now had the ability to destroy their planet. Some say this knowledge and power maintained peace during the Cold War. Both sides understood the balance of terror — if war began, the

World War II accelerated technological change in many fields, among them computer development. This picture shows the room-sized ENIAC computer at the Moore School of Electrical Engineering at the University of Pennsylvania, in 1946.

A large crowd gathers to watch an atomic bomb test in the Nevada desert during the 1950s. For long periods after World War II many people believed the world was on the brink of self-destruction. The U.S., Britain, some countries from the former USSR, France, and China are the recognized nuclear powers. Some other countries, such as India and North Korea admit to having nuclear weapons and it is suspected that several other countries, including Israel, also possess them.

destruction would be so great that neither side could possibly hope to win. Others say the development of atomic and related technologies has left a shadow hanging over the world which not even the ending of the Cold War can dispel.

Atomic research has also led to developments in other, more peaceful, areas. The most obvious has been the appearance of atomic power stations for the production of electricity without using finite fossil resources or generating harmful greenhouse gases. The first atomically generated electric power came on line at Schenectady, New York, in 1955. Other benefits from the atomic energy program included nuclear powered ships and advances in radiotherapy and radiography.

Other wartime scientific and technological projects, which had important consequences for the postwar world, included the development of radar ("radio detection and ranging"), antibiotic drugs, and the electronic computer. The British had developed radar to enable their defenses to detect incoming German bombers. In 1940 the device was in its infancy. Within ten years, thanks to the attention given to the concept during the war, it had become a crucial defense and navigational aid. Penicillin had been discovered in 1928, but here, too, the needs of war increased the pace of research. Antibiotic drugs were available for treating the Allied wounded at the Normandy landings in 1944. Military requirements also put pressure on scientists to hasten the appearance of the electronic computer. Among the first of these were the Mark I, developed at Harvard University in 1942, and the Colossus computers, which were developed in England to decipher messages from the German Enigma coding machines. Computers, like many other spin-offs from the war, are so much part of our modern civilization that it is difficult to imagine life without them.

A high-tech computerized aircraft instrument panel demonstrates the benefits of postwar advances in computer and radar technology. The lower image is a radar weather map; the white arced gauge above this is a compass, showing the aircraft heading (white triangle). The upper image shows runway approach information.

The technology of flight made a similarly rapid advance during the war. The main changes happened in four fields: speed, size, range, and the means of propulsion. Shortly after the war, as a direct consequence of research done while the fighting was still in progress, fighter aircraft appeared capable of flying faster than the speed of sound. From them grew a whole range of new airplanes, including the supersonic Anglo-French Concorde passenger aircraft. The requirements of the wartime bomber led to the development of huge, high-flying passenger airliners, such as the Stratocruiser, which could

World War II may have ended military conflict on a global scale. But we are no nearer peace. Assisting famine victims in Ethiopia in 1987, singer Bob Geldof complained that "Food is being used as a weapon of war."

travel immense distances without refueling. Larger planes were cheaper to operate, so more people could fly. Within a few decades, ordinary tourists were taking off for destinations their grandparents had hardly heard of.

Much of this was made possible by the jet engine, developed simultaneously in Britain and Germany, and first fitted to interceptor fighters. The pilotless bomb, or rocket, soon followed. German rocket technology developed by Werner von Braun to launch the V1 and V2 rockets against England during the war, formed the basis of the postwar U.S. space program. Braun took his entire development team to the United States and played a crucial role in preparing the Saturn rocket which made possible the U.S. Apollo 11 moon landing in 1969.

ONE PLANET

In 1985 the rock star Bob Geldof organized Live Aid, a massive concert to help African famine relief. It was watched by about one third of the total world population. No other fact better illustrates the meaning of the phrase "global village," a term often applied to the postwar world. All nations and all cultures are inter-linked in a way never thought necessary, possible, or desirable in the past.

This change has not come about just as a result of World War II. Indeed, superficially the Cold War divided people rather than brought them together. But the war did serve to speed up change. The very fact that, unlike World War I, it really was a world-wide conflict, forced people to think in global terms. The technology developed during the war enabled ideas, messages, pictures, and music to be transmit-ted from one part of the Earth's surface to another in seconds. It allowed people and goods to move around almost as quickly. The wonder of space flight allowed us for the first time to see ourselves as we really are — one species, on one planet, alone.

It was almost inevitable that with the improve-ment of communications there would be a gradual coming-together of cultures. The Cold War speeded up this process, as each side strove to present its philoso-phy and aims in the best possible light. In this con-test, the West won hands down. What it had to offer was so much more exciting and appealing than the drab uniformity and tired commonplaces of Soviet Communism. Through Hollywood the world already knew a good deal about Western, particularly U.S., culture. Television continued the process. It is said that the migration pattern of the people of the Sahara, unchanged for hundreds of years, altered in the 1970s to allow the nomads to view the TV soap opera *Dallas*. United States Information Service offices opened in most major cities throughout the world. American aid was offered to all who declared themselves anti-Communist. American Peace Corps volunteers traveled abroad to help the disadvantaged and underprivileged. Everyone claimed American-style human rights, and even the most tyrannical of dictators felt it necessary to call his or her rule "demo-cratic."

Before long there was hardly a city in the world where Western dress was not the norm for the up-and-coming. The English language spread like an epi-demic. Jeans, first worn by some Americans as work clothes, became a truly international article of cloth-ing. Weeks after miniskirts first appeared on the streets of London in the 1960s, they were adorning the thighs of the daring in almost every corner of the globe. Western pop music — instantly appealing, sen-

I believe that this nation should com-mit itself to achieving the goal, before this decade is out, of landing a man on the moon and returning him safely to Earth. No single project in this period will be more exciting, or more impressive to mankind, or more important for the long-range explo-ration of space; and none will be so diffi-cult or expensive to accomplish.

President Kennedy, May 1961.

Coca-Cola guzzling in Korea. One of the most noticeable consequences of World War II has been the spread of the American way of life around the world. For better or worse, there is now hardly a corner of the world where one cannot find cola, soap operas, and blue jeans.

sual, and tinged with the thrill of adolescent rebellion — blared from a million speakers on every continent. From Bombay to Bogota, children chased foreign tourists in the streets asking for chewing gum.

It is small wonder that some observers looked with horror at what was going on, and termed it "cultural imperialism." Never, in the aftermath of any war, had the victors imposed their way of life on their enemy so comprehensively, so gently, or with so little resistance.

THE LONG VIEW

In 1918 the victors of World War I surveyed the shattered lands of Western Europe and determined that that conflagration would be, in the future popular phrase, the war to end all wars. President Woodrow Wilson, Prime Minister Lloyd George of Britain, President Georges Clemenceau of France, and the governments they led, dictated peace treaties and set up institutions which they hoped would guarantee secure nation states, free from aggression from their neighbors. The prevailing mood was optimistic, the forecast from commentators upbeat.

Within 21 years Europe was at war again. In the

next few years the major powers joined battle to the extent of causing a genuine global war and at a level of intensity never before witnessed. When peace emerged again, the victors this time were chastened. The world order that emerged was fragile and hesitant. Frequently the United Nations was compared by skeptics to the ill-fated League of Nations in the 1930s. It was feared it would be only a matter of time before the world would be plunged into a new war, a conflict so devastating as to be quite definitely the final act.

And yet this has not happened — so far. Historians cannot predict the future, and the 21st century is bound to bring its share of disasters, both natural and created by human beings. Nevertheless, the world has been without a major war, on the scale of the two this century, for 50 years. Taking the long historical view this is an achievement of some note. World War II did involve gigantic losses, but also produced less evident gains. The most important of these is that people today can look forward to the future with more confidence than preceding generations.

For the first time, because the people of the world want peace and the leaders of the world are afraid of war, the times are on the side of peace.

The greatest honor history can bestow is the title of peacemaker. This honor now beckons America — the chance to help lead the world at last out of the valley of turmoil and on to that high ground of peace that man has dreamed of since the dawn of civilization . . . .

From the inaugural address of President Richard Nixon, January 1969.

Astronaut "Buzz" Aldrin salutes the American flag on the moon in 1969. After the war, Werner von Braun, former director of German military rocket research, went to the United States where he played a vital part in developing the missile technology that led to the successful U.S. moon landing 24 years later.

GLOSSARY

absolute
Complete or total.

Allies, the
The U.S., Britain, and other countries that fought together against the Axis during World War II.

appeasement
The policy of pacifying an enemy by giving way to some of their demands.

Axis
The alliance of Germany, Japan, Italy, Hungary, and other countries during World War II.

bloc
A group of nations that unite to further a common interest or purpose.

Bolsheviks
The group of Communists that seized power in Russia in 1917.

Camp David
Located in Maryland, an official retreat of the President of the U.S., where regular business and important conferences take place. President Roosevelt and Prime Minister Churchill held an important meeting here in 1943.

capitalism
The economic system based on free enterprise.

censorship
The practice of supressing ideas or materials considered objectionable by those in power.

civil war
War fought between opposing groups of people of one country.

communism
A system that holds that all goods should be held in common and that there should be no private property.

coup
The overthrow of a government by force.

democracy
Government by the people or their elected representatives.

dictator
An all-powerful ruler.

economy
A country's finances, services, and industry.

embargo
A legal ban on trading in certain goods.

empire
A widespread group of territories under the same government.

Fascism
Political system that stresses nationalism and often a particular race over the individual and other races; usually led by a dictator.

foreign policy
A state's policy toward other states.

global
Affecting the whole world.

guerrilla
A soldier who takes part in irregular warfare, often fighting in opposition to the government.

ideology
A way of thinking about social and political ideas, theories, and aims followed by a particular nation or group, e.g., capitalism, socialism, communism.

imperial
Relating to an empire.

Iron Curtain
The political frontier between Communist and capitalist Europe after 1946.

left wing
Inclined toward Socialism or liberalism.

liberalism
The political belief that emphasizes the individual and his or her civil and political liberties.

nationalism
A strong feeling of support for one's own country.

nonaligned
In neither the Western nor the Eastern sphere of influence.

occupy
To take over a state or territory.

pact
Formal agreement.

plebiscite
Direct vote by the electorate of a country on an important public question.

puppet state
Country that is nominally independent but actually under the control of a greater power.

propaganda
Information designed to promote one point of view.

recession
Economic downturn.

Red
Communist.

refugees
Homeless and stateless persons.

Reichstag
German parliament.

reparations
Payments by a defeated nation to meet the costs of a war and war damages.

republic
Country without a monarch, but with an elected head of state.

revolution
Complete and rapid change in a nation's political organization.

right wing
Inclined toward capitalism.

sanctions
Steps taken usually by other nations to make a state do something, but stopping short of military force.

slump
Deep recession.

socialism
A political system that stresses welfare and equality above profit and individualism.

Soviet
Elected council in a Communist nation. Used to describe anything of the former USSR.

superpower
A very powerful nation, usually meaning the United States or the former USSR.

state
A self-governing territory, usually a country.

USSR
The Union of Soviet Socialist Republics, formed in 1922, dissolved in 1991.

Vichy
Puppet French government in control of the southern portion of the country after the capitulation of France to the Germans in 1940.

FURTHER READING

Adler, David. *We Remember the Holocaust.* Holt, 1989

Allen, Peter. *The Origins of World War II.* Franklin Watts, 1992

Black, Wallace B. and Blashfield, Jean F. *America Prepares for War.* Macmillan, 1991
—— *Guadalcanal.* Macmillan, 1992

Bosco, Peter. *World War I.* Facts on File, 1991

Chrisp, Peter. *The Rise of Fascism.* Franklin Watts, 1991

Cross, Robin. *Roosevelt: And the Americans at War.* Franklin Watts, 1990

Devaney, John. *America Storms the Beaches.* Walker, 1993

Finkelstein, Norman. *Douglas MacArthur: The Emperor General: A Biography of Douglas MacArthur.* Macmillan, 1989

Grant, Neil. *Heroes of World War II.* Raintree Steck-Vaughn, 1990

Heater, Derek. *Cold War.* Franklin Watts, 1989

Hills, Ken. *1930s,* "Take Ten Years" series. Raintree Steck-Vaughn, 1992
—— *1940s,* "Take Ten Years" series. Raintree Steck-Vaughn, 1992

Marrin, Albert. *Hitler.* Puffin Books, 1993

Miller, Marilyn. *D-Day.* Silver Burdett Press, 1986

Mulvihill, Margaret. *Mussolini: And Italian Fascism.* Franklin Watts, 1990

O'Neal, Michael. *President Truman and the Atomic Bomb: Opposing Viewpoints.* Greenhaven Press, 1990

Reynolds, Floria. *Women at War.* Thomson Learning, 1993

Ross, Stewart. *United Nations.* Franklin Watts, 1990

Stewart, Gail. *World War I.* Lucent Books, 1991

Vail, John. *World War Two: The War in Europe.* Lucent Books, 1991

Weatherford, Doris. *American Women and World War Two.* Facts on File, 1990

Whitman, Sylvia. *V Is for Victory: The American Homefront During World War II.* Lerner, 1992

TIMELINE

1917 — The Bolshevik Communists come to power in Russia after overthrowing the government of the czar.

1918 — World War I ends.

1919 — The Treaty of Versailles is signed.

1920 — The League of Nations is formed.

1922 — Mussolini comes to power in Italy.

1924 — The Dawes Plan to ease German reparations is presented.

1925 — The Locarno Pact guarantees European frontiers.

1926 — Germany is admitted to League of Nations.

1928 — Stalin dominates the government in the USSR. Jiang Jieshi's Nationalists (GMD) take over in China. The Kellogg-Briand Pact renounces war.

1929 — The Young Plan to ease reparations further is presented. The Wall Street crash starts a world economic slump.

1930 — France begins to build the Maginot Line (to 1935).

1931 — Japan takes over the Chinese province of Manchuria.

1933 — Japan leaves the League of Nations. Hitler becomes chancellor of Germany, which leaves League of Nations.

1934 — Germany and Poland sign a non-aggression treaty. USSR joins the League of Nations.

1935 — Germany begins openly rearming. The Saar region rejoins Germany. Italian troops invade Abyssinia. League of Nations sanctions prove ineffective.

1936 — Britain increases defense expenditure. Civil war breaks out in Spain (to 1939). German troops enter the Rhineland unopposed. Rome-Berlin Axis is formed. Germany and Japan sign the Anti-Comintern Pact.

1937 — The Marco Polo Bridge incident takes place — Japan attacks China. Italy leaves League of Nations and joins Germany and Japan in Anti-Comintern Pact.

1938 — *Anschluss* of Germany and Austria takes place. The Czechoslovakian crisis is defused at Munich Conference. German troops enter the Sudetenland.

1939 — Czechoslovakia is occupied. Britain and France promise to uphold Polish independence. Hitler and Mussolini make a "Pact of Steel." Nazi-Soviet Non-Aggression Pact is signed. Germany invades Poland. Britain and France declare war on Germany. Soviet troops enter Poland and attack Finland — USSR is expelled from the League of Nations.

1940 — Germans attack Norway and Denmark, then Holland, France, and Belgium. Mussolini declares war on Britain and France. The Battle of Britain takes place. Germany, Japan, and Italy form a Tripartite Pact. Italy invades Greece.

1941 — The German invasion of the USSR takes place. Embargoes on sale of oil and steel to Japan are enacted. German forces are halted outside Moscow. Japanese attack Pearl Harbor — U.S. and Britain declare war on Japan; China declares war on Japan and Germany. Germany and Italy declare war on U.S.

1942 — The Wannsee Conference initiates the "Final Solution" to the "Jewish problem." Singapore falls to the Japanese. The Atlantic Charter is drawn up. The Mark I computer is built. The battles of Coral Sea and Midway take place. The battle of Guadalcanal takes place. The battles of Stalingrad (to 1943) and El Alamein take place.

1943 — The Allies land in Sicily and Italy. Italy leaves the war, then declares war on Germany. The Tehran Conference is held.

1944 — The U.S. invades the Marshall Islands. U.S. offensives begin on Saipan, Guam and Tinian. Soviet troops enter Poland. The D-Day Allied landings in Europe take place. The Battle of the Bulge is fought.

Dumbarton Oaks Conference sets out framework for the United Nations. Soviets enter Czechoslovakia and Hungary. U.S. forces land in the Philippines. Bombing of Japan begins.

1945 — The Yalta Conference is held. U.S. forces land on Okinawa. The Russians reach Berlin. Germany surrenders. The United Nations is formed. The Potsdam Conference is held. An atomic bomb is dropped on Hiroshima. USSR declares war on Japan. An atomic bomb is dropped on Nagasaki. Japan surrenders. Civil war breaks out in China. The Nuremberg Trials begin.

1946 — Poland and Hungary become Communist states. Churchill makes his "Iron Curtain" speech. Britain pulls out of Jordan.

1947 — India and Pakistan become independent. The Truman Doctrine is outlined. The Marshall Plan is put forward. Romania becomes a Communist state.

1948 — The formation of the state of Israel is declared; the Arab-Israeli war breaks out. Czechoslovakia becomes a Communist state. The Soviets begin a blockade of West Berlin (to 1949). A split opens up between Stalin of the USSR and Tito of Yugoslavia.

1949 — The USSR explodes its own atomic bomb. Germany formally splits into two countries. NATO is formed. The Chinese People's Republic (Communist) is proclaimed.

1950 — A treaty between USSR and China is signed. The "Iron Curtain" is made into a physical barrier (1950–1989).

1950-53 — The Korean War takes place.

1952 — A hydrogen bomb is tested by U.S.

1953 — Stalin dies. Anti-Communist riots take place in East Germany.

1954 — France is defeated by the Vietminh in Indochina. Vietnam is divided into the Communist north and anti-Communist south.

1955 — Arab-Israeli fighting begins (to 1956). The Warsaw Pact is formed. Austria's independence is restored.

1956 — A Hungarian revolt is crushed.

1957 — The European Economic Community is formed. Sputnik is launched.

1958 — The Chinese "Great Leap Forward"economic program is initiated.

1960 — The Sino-Soviet rift occurs.

1961 — Yuri Gagarin of the USSR becomes the first man in space. The Berlin Wall is built.

1962 — The Cuban missile crisis takes place.

1965 — U.S. troops become combatants in Vietnam (to 1973).

1966 — The Chinese Cultural Revolution begins (to 1969)

1967 — The Arab-Israeli Six-Day War is fought.

1968 — "Prague Spring" liberalization movement takes place in Czechoslovakia.

1969 — Two Americans are first humans to land on moon.

1971 — China takes Taiwan's seat in Security Council of the UN.

1972 — President Richard Nixon visits China.

1973 — Arab-Israeli Yom Kippur War is fought.

1978 — The Camp David Agreement ends Israeli-Egyptian hostility.

1985 — Mikhail Gorbachev comes to power in USSR.

1989-90 — The Communist empire in Eastern Europe collapses. The Cold War officially ends.

INDEX

ACKNOWLEDGMENTS

The publishers are grateful to the following for
permission to reproduce photographs:

Cover photo (large): UPI/Bettmann
Cover photo (small): Range/Bettmann
Weimar Archive, pages 6, 11, 18, 19, 21, 22, 23, 27, 28,
37, 42; Peter Newark's Military Pictures, pages 7, 11,
26, 39, 62; Hulton Deutsch Collection, pages 8, 24, 33,
52, 53, 61, 68; UPI/Bettmann, pages 12, 45, 48, 65;
Popperfoto, pages 15, 17, 20, 30, 46, 55, 66, 71; Imperial
War Museum, London, pages 29, 31; Range/Bettmann/
UPI, pages 32, 64; David King Collection, pages 40, 47,
54; Bettmann Archive, page 41; Range/Bettmann, page
49; United Nations, pages 56, 58, 59; United Nations/
Myrtle Winter Chaumeny, page 57; Dick Luria/Science
Photo Library, page 67; Tony Stone Worldwide, page 70.